LOVE LIKE YESHUA NOT LIKE ZEUS

A DEVOTIONAL

CHERYL A. DURHAM, PH.D.

Cover Art: Public Domain:
Christ by Heinrich Hofmann; Wikimedia Commons;
Zeus god of the sky; Camphalfblood.Wiki.com

Cover Design and Editing: Donna Dozier

Copyright © 2014 Cheryl Durham

All rights reserved.

ISBN-978-1497341111
ISBN-1497341116

Table of Contents

CHAPTER 1 - INTRODUCTION 1

HOW TO USE THIS BOOK 11

CHAPTER 2 - INQUIRY...13

CHAPTER 3 - INQUIRY: WEEK ONE........................17

CHAPTER 4 - INQUIRY: WEEK TWO........................21

CHAPTER 5 - INQUIRY: WEEK THREE 25

CHAPTER 6 - INQUIRY: WEEK FOUR 29

CHAPTER 7–INTEGRATION: WRESTLING WITH MY PARADIGM.....................................33

CHAPTER 8 - IMPLEMENTING CHANGE 41

CHAPTER 9 - CONCLUDING THOUGHTS..............43

VOCABULARY 45

CHAPTER 10 - RESOURCES..47

ABOUT THE AUTHOR...51

CHAPTER 1 - INTRODUCTION

When writing about Loving like Yeshua, I want you to know that I am not talking about the kind of love you hear about in sermons – the definitions from the GREEK language. I am not talking about the GREEK meaning of love in any of its forms. You may think that you are familiar with God's love because you have heard of words like 'agape' or 'phileo' or 'eros' because Christians are all familiar with these ideas from pastors who want to talk about Love using the Greek words.

However, when pastors stop their research with the use of the Greek lexicons, they are assuming that the Greek somehow has equivalence in language to the language that Yeshua and the Apostles spoke, which was Hebrew. Not only is the Greek not equal to the language that the Biblical writers used, in many cases Greek is oppositional to the worldview that the Bible writers held.

This is a wrong assumption and it leads to misinterpretation of the meaning of the text. Just finding what Greek word was used for another Hebrew word does not mean that the meanings are the same in both Greek and Hebrew.

If a pastor or teacher does this, he or she will miss the real meaning of the text. While there are several words for 'love' in Greek that have specific meanings, it is not so in Hebrew. Hebrew writers sometimes borrow words from Greek to express Hebrew meanings, but if one is not familiar with how the writers did this, the meaning of the passage is dulled and often wrong.

The fact that the people who wrote the text were NOT GREEK and that they were Hebrew may sound like a mere detail; it is not.

The fact of the matter is that the Greek idea of love is based on Greek ideas, Greek thinking and Greek gods like Zeus – not the God of Israel whom Christians claim to worship. The Hebrews use words like *ahav* and *ch̲esed* to allude to the action of covenant love, while the Greeks describe love as a feeling or a passive state of being. The New Testament writers are referring to the Hebrew verb *ahav* and its underlying structure of *ch̲esed*. The writers are not describing a feeling or a passive state of being when they write about love. To love like Yeshua requires covenant obligation that shows in our practice. It shows in our commitment to others who may or may not be like us.

Love in Hebrew is not just being nice or feeling love, it is returning the love, by following the commandments that God *expects* from His people because we owe him (*<u>ch</u>esed*). This is the same behavior that Yeshua expects from his followers because He says it is the sign of our love for Him. Keeping the covenant commandments is equal to love for His disciples (John 17).

This is a far cry from the idea that love is merely unselfish giving to others. Agape is used by the writers of the New Testament, to represent the concept of *ahav* which is a love that is tied to the Hebrew word *<u>ch</u>esed*. *<u>Ch</u>esed* is a relational word that describes the movement in a committed relationship – like a dance.

The Jewish people were not confused about the differences between Hebrew and Greek.

During the Hellenistic period, even before the first century, there were all kinds of conflicts going on with the different sects of Israel that revolved around sustaining the way of life that Israel, as the people of God, had lived for thousands of years.

The Greek culture was seen by *the purists*, as a dilution of the community life God had ordained in Torah. However, there were other sects, who wanted to participate more in Greek life, and believed that Hellenism could be integrated into the life of Israel without offending God. These sects were primarily from the Diaspora.

In this way, our current culture mimics the culture of that time. There are those who believe that we should follow the Bible as it has been practiced for thousands of years and there are those who believe that doing so would alienate us from the world. Christians in particular use this approach for evangelism. They want 'seekers' to come into the church. They want to 'plant' churches and 'grow' the numbers. These people believe that the church should accommodate and emulate the world. Christians should have something to offer that is attractive. So they try to fit in, like having "Christian concerts" or "Christian movies" or as George Barna says, *'Spiritainment'* which is a blend of spirituality and entertainment meant to attract nonbelievers[1].

Christians, who fear that people will not like them or not come into the church, attempt to 'fit in' with the current culture this way. Like the *Diaspora sects,* integration is important to them. Just like today, the Hebrew way of life in the time of Yeshua often conflicted with the world's way of doing things. God had asked His covenant people to be a people *'set apart'* for Him.

The Apostle Paul, whose ministry was, to a large extent, in the Diaspora, created mixed (Jew and Gentile) congregations. He tried to teach this mixed group how to do things more

---

[1] http://tinyurl.com/ldpj2hr

"Hebraically". He did this because he was familiar with the cultural issues during this time, and how difficult it would be to have Jews and Gentiles in the same community (Acts 10).

Paul, knowing the difficulty, attempted to integrate Jew and Gentile so that there would be both Jews and Gentiles in the people of God (Galatians 3). Despite popular opinion, he was not trying to integrate the Greek and Hebrew worldviews. Paul was converting Gentiles (many who were already *Godfearers* or *proselytes*) to the Jewish faith. He was not trying to convert Jews or tell them they did not have to follow Torah (Acts 15). Paul was trying to have Jews and Gentiles love one another just like Yeshua (the Jew – not the Greek) loved. He was not trying to integrate Yeshua with the Greek god, Zeus. The people in

Love Like Yeshua, Not Like Zeus

Paul's community were very familiar with how one loved the Greek and Roman gods. We see this in the conflicts Paul had in his congregations. It was the Hebrew idea, *ahav* and <u>*chesed*</u> that they needed to apply to their community. For them, it was a new way of seeing. Translation of languages can be difficult. The cultural meaning of words and phrases can be even more difficult to trace.

In talking about how to *Love like Yeshua*, we have to consider the Hebrew view of the time and the meaning of the text to the first audience, like the people in Paul's ministry. If you read the last <u>devotional,</u> you will, by now, understand that Yeshua was Jewish – and totally Torah-observant. So in order to understand how God loves and how He expects us to love, we have to

Love Like Yeshua, Not Like Zeus

understand the Hebrew view. This applies to the people of God. Remember, Paul said, there is neither Jew nor Greek, male nor female (Galatians); we are all the same 'in Christ'. To love like Yeshua, we have to remember too that Yeshua ONLY did what the Father told Him to do or what He saw the Father do. He did not represent Himself; he only followed the Father. So we have to look at what God means by love as revealed in Torah, so we can see how Yeshua loved. In the next three devotionals, we will compare and contrast the Hebrew idea of love with the Greek, and hopefully you'll begin to see the major difference.

Shalom,

HOW TO USE THIS BOOK

Work on one verse a week. Read these verses and answer the questions. If you come up with more questions than answers, GOOD!

Write them in the notes section so you can research them. Look up the links and reference materials and take notes on what you learn.

I am available by email! If you have a few people who would like to have a conference on this, let me know and we can work something out.

You can email me at Cheryl@livingtruth.us

Love Like Yeshua, Not Like Zeus

CHAPTER 2 - INQUIRY

What is the most important word in Scripture?

Simple Answer: חסד (*chesed*)

The most important word in Scripture that tells us about God is the word *chesed* (חסד). *Chesed* is a word that is unique to Hebrew, and no other languages in the Ancient Near East have any cognates that compare to this word. In fact, this word is so difficult to translate that it is translated with many words such as *eleos* (mercy), *dikaiosyne* (righteous or just) and *charis* (grace) and others – with none of them incorporating all of the facets of what *chesed* means.

Love Like Yeshua, Not Like Zeus

How in the world are we to understand God if we don't have words to describe what He is? Well, in Hebrew, it's about ACTION. So let's look at God's love through His actions. What we see about *ch*esed is that it is unique, that it is permanent, and that it is reliable. Those are the qualities that must underlie love; permanence and reliability. Love at its base is commitment.

To understand *ch*esed is to know that it contains 4 facets that all function at the same time. **Chesed is Relational, Reciprocal, Transitive, and Active, all at once**[i]. *Ch*esed is like a wheel that goes around and forward at the same time.

In the study this month we will explore each facet of *ch*esed. It is the way God loves. There is an understood obligation for all who enter into a relationship with God through Yeshua that requires a mutual commitment to *do chesed*.

In order to understand how to love like Yeshua, we need to understand the character of God. As Yeshua said, he does nothing of himself, rather only what the Father tells him to do. This tells us that Yeshua did not see himself as an individual; he saw himself as part of the purposes of God. Israel, as God's people are the vehicle through which God's light is shone. Yeshua, as the representative of Israel, does that perfectly.

Loving like Yeshua means that we will make a permanent and reliable commitment to the community life of the people of God. *Chesed* is *only* through

Love Like Yeshua, Not Like Zeus

that commitment to God. Not exactly a precise Greek description, is it?

CHAPTER 3 - INQUIRY: WEEK ONE

Chesed is Relational

Verse: Psalm 136:1-26

"Give thanks to the LORD, for he is good; For his lovingkindness endures forever."

You can find this Psalm here[2] or read it in the Bible of your choice. I chose the HNV because it is sensitive to the Hebraic names and phrases during the time of Yeshua.

When you read this psalm, see how David continually repeats how God is

---

[2] http://www.blueletterbible.org/Bible.cfm?b=Psa&c=136&t=HNV

faithful to His people Israel. David continually reminds the children of Israel how much they 'owe' God.

Week One Questions:

1. How does David's description of God's faithfulness show his relationship to His people Israel?

2. In what ways does David imply that Israel 'owes' God something in return?

3. What is it that David believes that the people of Israel owe God?

4. How does this psalm recall God's Creation in Genesis 1?

5. What is significant about God's creation and a covenant relationship with His people? Who does God take care of? Why?

Love Like Yeshua, Not Like Zeus

CHAPTER 4 - INQUIRY: WEEK TWO

Chesed is Reciprocal

Verse: Psalm 103

"Praise the LORD, my soul, And don't forget all his benefits"

Very often, when we think about 'grace' which in Hebrew is *hen,* we think about *agape* love or what we believe to be unconditional love. It is compassion for the 'other'. Unconditional love is not connected to an obligation. That is what *unconditional* means. It follows that when God gives us 'grace', and we accept it, that there is no further obligation. However, that understanding of the word *agape* requires a Greek, and not Hebrew, meaning.

In the Hebraic view, when one accepts the grace (*hen*), he or she is also accepting the reciprocal obligation. With *hen* comes <u>ch</u>*esed*, and <u>ch</u>*esed* implies a *communal* obligation. It is the reciprocal obligation that believers have to God and His community which, when we invite God into our lives through Yeshua, becomes our community as well. *There is **one** community in Christ. (Ga. 3:28)*

<u>Ch</u>*esed* needs to be *reciprocal* to show that a relationship exists. Our *showing* <u>ch</u>*esed* toward God and our neighbor tells the world that we are part of God's community, by choice. It's a matter of faithfulness.

As we saw last week, God is always faithful. In return for His kindness to us, He expects our *mutual faithfulness* to Him, and through Him, to His community. How do we show it? Through praise of Him; and how do we praise Him? We praise God by showing *hen* to others in the hope that they will choose to be part of God's people too. This is evangelism! – not *'belief'* in a person, but action in a community. *Belief* is Greek; *action* is Hebrew. Yeshua is Jewish, not Greek. To love like Yeshua is to practice <u>ch</u>*esed*, as part of the community of God.

Love Like Yeshua, Not Like Zeus

Week Two Questions:

1. Does your congregation practice communal obligation toward God's community of Jews and Gentiles that make up the body of Christ?

2. What does your congregation say to a new believer? Is he/she obligated to the community? Why or why not?

3. Does your congregation practice the praise of God by commitment to the community? Why or Why not?

4. How do verses 17-18 model your community experience?

5. If things need to change, what are they?

CHAPTER 5 - INQUIRY: WEEK THREE

Chesed is Transitive

Verse: Matthew 22:36-40

"Teacher, which is the greatest mitzvah in the law? Yeshua said to him, You shall love the Lord your God with all your heart, and with all your soul, and with all your mind. This is the first and great mitzvah. A second likewise is this, You shall love your neighbor as yourself. The whole law and the prophets depend on these two mitzvot."

Yeshua quoted the Shema, which identified Him with the community of Israel. He did not set a *'new law'*; he was quoting an old one. (Deuteronomy 6 and Lev. 19:18)

Love Like Yeshua, Not Like Zeus

In this verse, Yeshua isn't saying anything new. He is telling His people Israel that what they do matters. The Shema is in Deuteronomy 6 and it is a prayer said daily by devout Jews. This was not a surprise. Additionally, Leviticus 19 tells the people of Israel that they are to love their neighbor as themselves. None of this is new, so why is Yeshua telling us this? Perhaps for our ears as well. When we love God we are to be faithful to the covenant. We are not just to have nice feelings about God. If you love Him, says Yeshua in John 17, we need to obey His commandments. Love equals obedience. That is not the meaning of *agape*. It's the meaning of <u>ch</u>esed. To do <u>ch</u>esed is to be faithful to God and to reach out to others for God, not in the hopes of manipulating them to believe what you do; rather it is to show them what the community is like, without an agenda. This is a very different view of evangelism.

Love Like Yeshua, Not Like Zeus

Week Three Questions:

1. Look up the word 'transitive'. How do Yeshua's words model this idea?

2. How does Yeshua identify with Israel in this passage?

3. How does obedience make the case for love?

4. How does Yeshua show His love for Israel? Is He insisting that they believe Him? Why or Why not?

5. Can you see that this is not an evangelical message compatible with 21st-century Christian evangelical ideas?

6. Why not?

CHAPTER 6 - INQUIRY: WEEK FOUR

Chesed is Always Active in the community

Verse: Luke 10:30-37

He said, "He who showed mercy on him." Then Yeshua said to him, "Go and do likewise."

Yeshua believed that all community members have an obligation to God to love others.

Yeshua is the best example of *chesed*. He loved God by following Torah perfectly; He loved others by sacrificing himself for them. He loved Israel because to be part of Israel is to represent the whole of Israel before God. Because of this, He accepted whatever consequences resulted. Yeshua knew that *ch*esed is *relational, reciprocal, transitive and active,* and that it involves obligation – not just nice feelings. In this passage we see that even the Samaritan, who was not Jewish, or formally part of Israel to Israel, felt the obligation to do what God commanded of the community. The Samaritan practiced Torah. He was observant to the Law, even without the benefit of Israel's covenant with God. How does this compare with merely an 'unselfish' love? Unconditional love (the meaning of agape) does not fit here. The Samaritan obeys the law by loving God through loving his neighbor. *Ch*esed is the better description for this concept – so how do you love?

Questions:

1. Why does the Samaritan feel the obligation to serve without covenant?

2. How does 'compassion' fit in with the obligation toward _chesed_?

3. How does *unconditional love* (agape) fall short of the full meaning of _chesed_?

4. Do you see now that using merely Greek words to understand Scripture is faulty?

5. What things have you learned from this verse?

Love Like Yeshua, Not Like Zeus

CHAPTER 7–INTEGRATION: WRESTLING WITH MY PARADIGM

When we read the Bible in English, and we understand that the NT documents were written in Greek, we often do not think about the enormous difficulties in conveying meaning that can occur, not only through translation, but through culture over time as well.

The Greek Language is not *merely* another language that has words that mirror the Hebrew Language. The Greek and the Hebrew Worldviews were very different and the Greek words used in the NT were often used to communicate Hebrew terms. The Greek idea of love is one such concept. In fact, *agape* was a relatively unused word at the time of the writing of the Septuagint (LXX). *Agape* was reincarnated in the LXX to be used to describe the love God has for His people. God's love is faithful and covenantal; it is love with a communal context. More importantly it is not 'unconditional' in the Greek sense of the word. Therefore we cannot look at the classical definition of *agape* for the meaning used by the New Testament authors. They were trying to communicate the word love in Hebrew *ahav* which derives from the idea of love within the concept of *chesed*. *A covenant is conditional.* Therefore, *agape*, as *unconditional* does not really capture the Hebrew meaning.

What we have learned through understanding *chesed* is that God does have expectations of His people. Yeshua, being part of Israel, knew that; so did Paul. Their view of love had to encompass the view of what covenant love was, and the role that obligation played in the meaning.

Questions:

In the following sections, write your thoughts and questions.

When reading the New Testament, it is important to understand that I am reading a translation that is thousands of years distant from the original written documents. In addition, my culture has changed even in my lifetime, and so it is unlikely that the culture that Yeshua lived in is similar to mine or even the Greek culture that Yeshua's orthodox Jewish community would embrace. Therefore, I need to try to understand at least the important concepts of the Bible through the ears of the first audiences so that I can accurately discern where there may be meaning for me in the 21st century.

It is unlikely that when Yeshua

used the word love (and Yeshua spoke Hebrew, not Greek) that he would use it in His context and not in the context of the Greek culture that the orthodox Jewish people of His time eschewed. The Apostle Paul, however, used the Greek language but not the way most Christians have been taught to believe. Starting to understand these concepts opens the door to a deeper, more intimate relationship with Yeshua and Torah, and it widens the ability to see others through God's eyes.

Love Like Yeshua, Not Like Zeus

Personal Reflection:

How does this affect my thinking about God?

How do I think about Yeshua now? Who is He?

How do I think about the things Yeshua says? Have they been 'Christianized'?

Love Like Yeshua, Not Like Zeus

What does God think about what the Church has done with His covenant/people?

Should all this knowledge influence my walk?

Love Like Yeshua, Not Like Zeus

CHAPTER 8 - IMPLEMENTING CHANGE

Gained knowledge is only helpful when we implement change.

As a result of what you learned this month think about the following things, and what you will do with what you learned!

How should this make an impact on my walk?

What needs to change? What does that look like?

Conclusion

More questions: Learning always creates more questions. Write them here so that you can come back to them later.

1.

2.

3.

4.

CHAPTER 9 - CONCLUDING THOUGHTS

Simply Share what you have learned~

What Have I Learned about chesed and agape?

_____
_____
_____
_____
_____
_____
_____
_____
_____
_____
_____
_____
_____
_____
_____
_____

Love Like Yeshua, Not Like Zeus

Vocabulary

Agape

Chesed

Hen

Covenant

Love Like Yeshua, Not Like Zeus

CHAPTER 10 - RESOURCES

Books

The book of Ruth in the Bible

The story of Rahab in the Bible

Websites

Skip Moen on Chesed

http://skipmoen.com/?s=hesed

Paper on Chesed

http://www.graftedinfellowship.org/uploads/5/7/3/3/5733440/study_of_the_word_love.pdf

Derek Lehman on Chesed:

http://www.derekleman.com/musings/hesed-in-the-bible/

Love Like Yeshua, Not Like Zeus

Ideas to investigate:

The word *Chesed*

http://scholar.google.com/scholar?q=%22hesed%22+in+the+bible&btnG=&hl=en&as_sdt=0%2C31

The next two devotionals will further explore this concept by digging into the Greek idea of *agape* and how the two concepts overlap, or perhaps clash.

Love Like Yeshua, Not Like Zeus

ABOUT THE AUTHOR

Cheryl is a wife, mother, grandmother, entrepreneur, and author. She has been a Biblical Facilitator since 1996, and is currently on the Board of Trustees of Living Truth serving as Board Liaison to Ministries. You can contact Cheryl by email: drcdurham@gmail.com

She has a Master's degree in Biblical Counseling, and a Doctor of Biblical Studies in Contemporary Apologetics and Theology, and a Ph.D. in Theology from the Master's Theological Research Institute where she is also on staff. Her website and virtual classroom can be found at www.livingtruthnetwork.com where Biblical Facilitators and distance- learning students can find resources and encouragement.

To contact Dr. Durham
Email: Cheryl@livingtruth.us

---

[i] Skip Moen has excellent resources for this. Here are four videos < http://vimeo.com/album/2569229> that can help you get started. (Moen, Bib. WV 2)

Made in the USA
Charleston, SC
31 March 2014